WWE EPIC BATTLES IN 3-D

BY JAKE BLACK

📖 **SCHOLASTIC**

© 2012 becker&mayer! LLC

Published by Tangerine Press, an imprint of Scholastic Inc.,

557 Broadway, New York, NY 10012

Scholastic Canada Ltd., Markham, Ontario

WWE Epic Battles in 3-D is produced by becker&mayer! LLC

11120 NE 33rd Place, Suite 101

Bellevue, WA 98004

www.beckermayer.com

Published by arrangement with Grosset & Dunlap, a division of Penguin Young Readers Group, a member of Penguin Group (USA) Inc.

If you have questions or comments about this product, please visit www.beckermayer.com/customerservice and click on Customer Service Request Form.

Author: Jake Black

Editor: Betsy Henry Pringle

Designer: Sam Dawson

Production coordinator: Jennifer Marx

Photo researcher: Katie del Rosario

3-D anaglyph designers: Matt Fisher, Lena Kartzov, Kathy Thopmson, and Bill Whitaker

Managing editor: Amelia Riedler

Printed, manufactured, and assembled in Dongguan, China

10 9 8 7 6 5 4 3 2 1

ISBN: 978-0-545-52252-6

12269

LEGENDARY WWE BRAWLERS BATTLE IT OUT IN EYE-POPPING 3-D!

Step into the ring with the baddest brawlers of WWE! All the action is right here, right now, and in your face in breathtaking 3-D. Feel the heat as legendary WWE Superstars and Divas struggle to maintain supremacy. Discover their backstories, special moves, and strategies, and then study their stats to compare the masters of mayhem.

THE MATCHUPS

JOHN CENA vs. BROCK LESNAR

Superstars Collide

For years, John Cena was the biggest Superstar in WWE. Brock Lesnar was a champion in Mixed Martial Arts (MMA). The collision of these two Goliaths was destined to rock the planet. Lesnar, returning to the WWE after an eight-year absence, attacked Cena on his first night back. He vowed he would take out the WWE's brightest star. Lesnar knew he was strong and ruthless enough to destroy Cena.

The match was epic. Two mighty Superstars on a collision course toward destruction. Lesnar lunged at Cena, pummeling him with blow after blow. Cena broke free, landing a few kicks, but Lesnar recovered quickly—faster than Cena was expecting. Catching Cena off guard, Lesnar hoisted the leader of the Cenation onto his shoulders and whipped him around in a devastating F-5 slam. As he was gloating over Cena's fallen body, Lesnar failed to notice that his challenger had recovered from the slam. Grabbing Lesnar from behind, Cena pinned him to the mat and nailed the win!

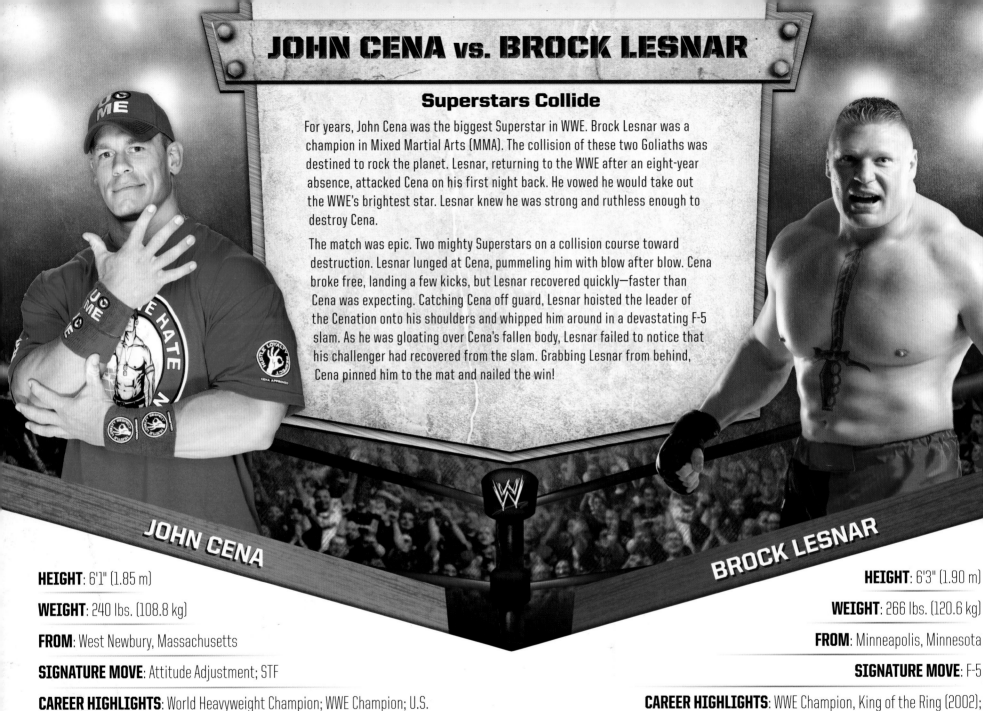

JOHN CENA

HEIGHT: 6'1" (1.85 m)

WEIGHT: 240 lbs. (108.8 kg)

FROM: West Newbury, Massachusetts

SIGNATURE MOVE: Attitude Adjustment; STF

CAREER HIGHLIGHTS: World Heavyweight Champion; WWE Champion; U.S. Champion; World Tag Team Champion; WWE Tag Team Champion; Royal Rumble Winner (2008)

BROCK LESNAR

HEIGHT: 6'3" (1.90 m)

WEIGHT: 266 lbs. (120.6 kg)

FROM: Minneapolis, Minnesota

SIGNATURE MOVE: F-5

CAREER HIGHLIGHTS: WWE Champion, King of the Ring (2002); Royal Rumble Winner (2003)

CM PUNK vs. DANIEL BRYAN

The Two Best in the World

For nearly ten years, CM Punk and Daniel Bryan competed in small sports entertainment promotions worldwide. Each man refined his skills, finally making it to WWE's grand stage. The two were on separate, but similar, paths leading to the pinnacle of the WWE. Bryan captured the World Heavyweight Championship. Punk won the WWE Championship. Punk declared he was the "Best in the World." Bryan disagreed—he was determined to prove his tattooed rival was wrong. Only a classic wrestling match could settle the matter.

Bryan and Punk have similar styles, so they know each other's moves and counter moves. Neither man had a clear advantage in the ring. When Bryan locked Punk in the "Yes!" Lock, Punk countered and escaped. When Punk tried his trademark G.T.S., Bryan slipped out of it. Kicks and aerial moves were delivered by both parties. Finally, Bryan pinned Punk in a submission hold, only to have Punk twist it into a pin on Bryan. As the referee counted to three, a triumphant Bryan was sure that Punk had submitted, but Punk was declared the winner.

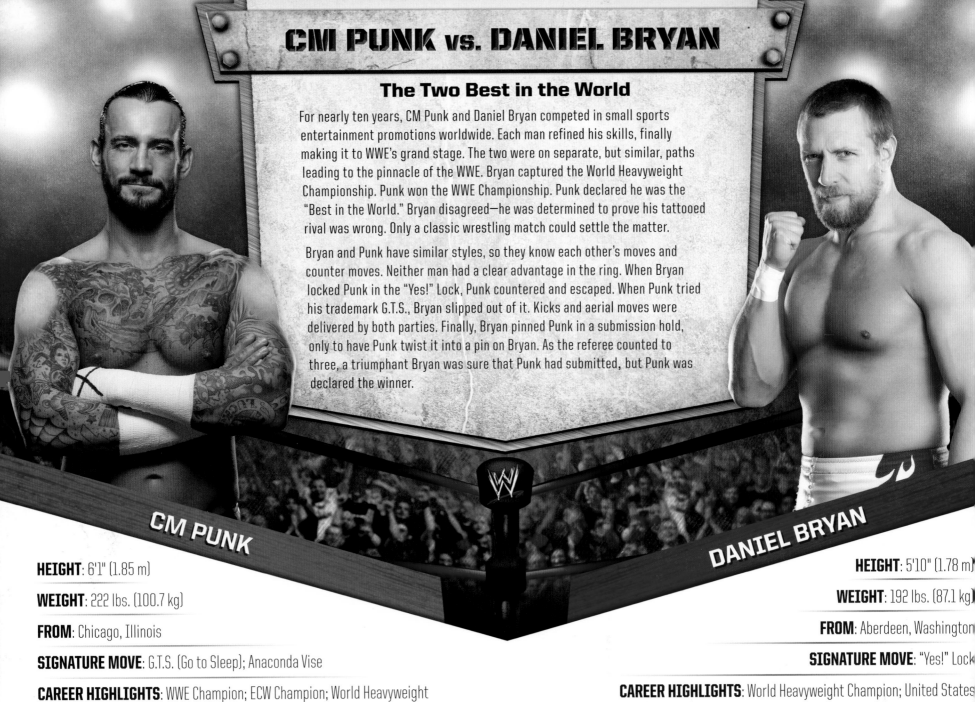

CM PUNK

HEIGHT: 6'1" (1.85 m)

WEIGHT: 222 lbs. (100.7 kg)

FROM: Chicago, Illinois

SIGNATURE MOVE: G.T.S. (Go to Sleep); Anaconda Vise

CAREER HIGHLIGHTS: WWE Champion; ECW Champion; World Heavyweight Champion; World Tag Team Champion; Intercontinental Champion

DANIEL BRYAN

HEIGHT: 5'10" (1.78 m)

WEIGHT: 192 lbs. (87.1 kg)

FROM: Aberdeen, Washington

SIGNATURE MOVE: "Yes!" Lock

CAREER HIGHLIGHTS: World Heavyweight Champion; United States Champion; SmackDown Money in the Bank Winner (2011); Trained by Shawn Michaels and William Regal

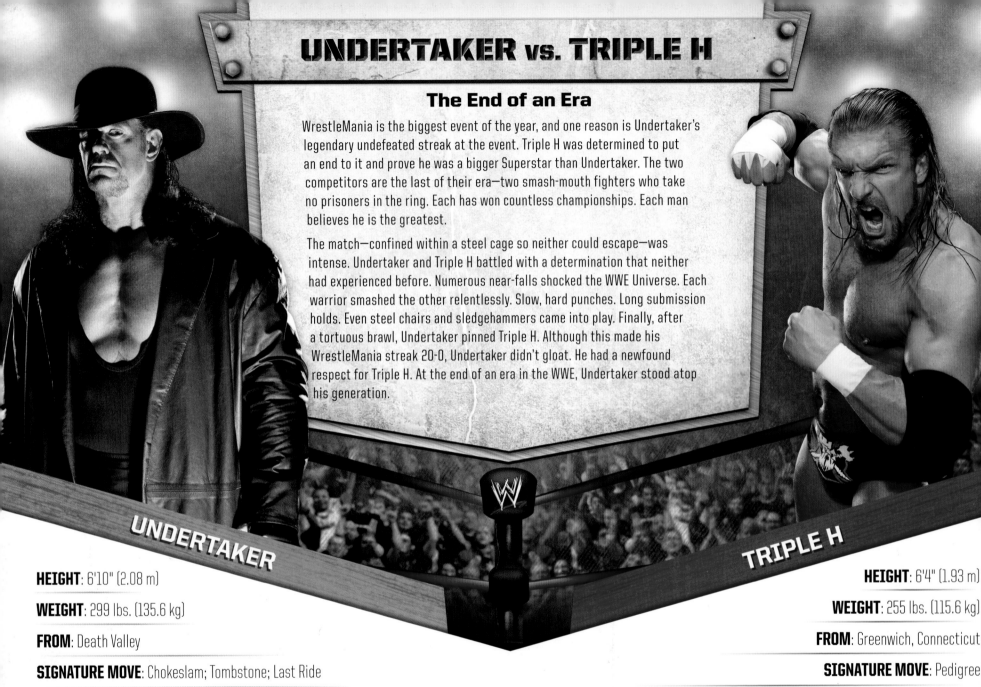

UNDERTAKER vs. TRIPLE H

The End of an Era

WrestleMania is the biggest event of the year, and one reason is Undertaker's legendary undefeated streak at the event. Triple H was determined to put an end to it and prove he was a bigger Superstar than Undertaker. The two competitors are the last of their era—two smash-mouth fighters who take no prisoners in the ring. Each has won countless championships. Each man believes he is the greatest.

The match—confined within a steel cage so neither could escape—was intense. Undertaker and Triple H battled with a determination that neither had experienced before. Numerous near-falls shocked the WWE Universe. Each warrior smashed the other relentlessly. Slow, hard punches. Long submission holds. Even steel chairs and sledgehammers came into play. Finally, after a tortuous brawl, Undertaker pinned Triple H. Although this made his WrestleMania streak 20-0, Undertaker didn't gloat. He had a newfound respect for Triple H. At the end of an era in the WWE, Undertaker stood atop his generation.

UNDERTAKER

HEIGHT: 6'10" (2.08 m)

WEIGHT: 299 lbs. (135.6 kg)

FROM: Death Valley

SIGNATURE MOVE: Chokeslam; Tombstone; Last Ride

CAREER HIGHLIGHTS: WWE Champion; World Heavyweight Champion; World Tag Team Champion; WCW Tag Team Champion; Hardcore Champion; WrestleMania Undefeated Streak (20-0)

TRIPLE H

HEIGHT: 6'4" (1.93 m)

WEIGHT: 255 lbs. (115.6 kg)

FROM: Greenwich, Connecticut

SIGNATURE MOVE: Pedigree

CAREER HIGHLIGHTS: WWE Chief Operating Officer; WWE Champion; World Heavyweight Champion; Intercontinental Champion; Unified WWE Tag Team Champion; World Tag Team Champion; European Champion; King of the Ring (1997); Royal Rumble Winner (2002)

SHEAMUS vs. ALBERTO DEL RIO

The Celtic Warrior Fights Mexican Royalty

Sheamus was the World Heavyweight Champion. Alberto Del Rio wanted to be. But Del Rio's dreams required that he defeat the Celtic Warrior—no simple task. The tough Irishman loved holding the World Heavyweight Title. Even if Del Rio relied on the assistance of his personal ring announcer, Ricardo Rodriguez, was he good enough to capture the championship? In the weeks before their match, Del Rio attacked Sheamus at every opportunity—backstage, in the parking lot, and even in the arena. He wanted to soften up Sheamus for their match.

The sneak attacks on Sheamus took their toll—it was beginning to look like "The Great White" might be in danger of losing his championship. Once the two brawlers were in the ring, Del Rio tried trick after trick to trap Sheamus. Rodriguez held Sheamus so Del Rio could attack. But this strategy backfired, and Del Rio socked his own ring announcer! Sheamus spun around, smashing the aristocratic Del Rio with a big Brogue Kick, knocking him to the mat. With a quick pin, Sheamus, victorious, retained his title.

SHEAMUS

HEIGHT: 6'6" (1.98 m)

WEIGHT: 272 lbs. (123.3 kg)

FROM: Dublin, Ireland

SIGNATURE MOVE: High Cross; Brogue Kick; Irish Curse

CAREER HIGHLIGHTS: World Heavyweight Champion; WWE Champion; U.S. Champion; King of the Ring (2010); Royal Tumble Winner (2012)

ALBERTO DEL RIO

HEIGHT: 6'5" (1.95 m)

WEIGHT: 263 lbs. (119.3 kg)

FROM: San Luis Potosi, Mexico

SIGNATURE MOVE: Cross Armbreaker

CAREER HIGHLIGHTS: WWE Champion; Royal Rumble Winner (2011); Raw Money in the Bank Winner (2011)

PRIMO vs. KOFI KINGSTON

High Flying Fighters

Primo and Kofi Kingston disliked each other and wanted to settle their differences in the ring. One match would show who the better brawler was. That is, after all, what WWE is all about—settling conflicts within the confines of the ring. Kingston had cheering fans behind him, while Primo was forced to rely on his own inner determination for motivation.

Both Superstars were high flyers with similar styles. They flew through the air, leaping off the top rope with kicks, dives, and big splashes. Kingston appeared to be in control of the match. He'd had more experience in singles competition. Primo had spent most of his WWE career as a member of a tag team. But Primo was a sneaky competitor, and while Kingston wasn't looking, he climbed to the top rope and dove off, hitting his opponent with a flying clothesline. Kingston couldn't recover from the blow in time, and Primo pinned him, nailing the win.

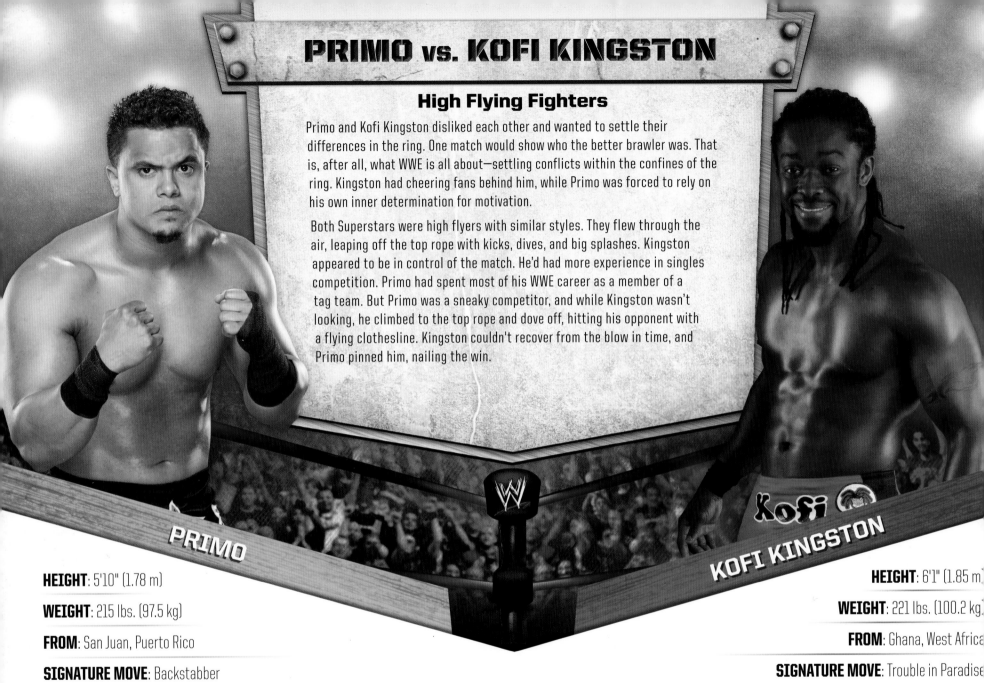

PRIMO

HEIGHT: 5'10" (1.78 m)

WEIGHT: 215 lbs. (97.5 kg)

FROM: San Juan, Puerto Rico

SIGNATURE MOVE: Backstabber

CAREER HIGHLIGHTS: WWE Tag Team Champion; Unified Tag Team Champion

KOFI KINGSTON

HEIGHT: 6'1" (1.85 m)

WEIGHT: 221 lbs. (100.2 kg)

FROM: Ghana, West Africa

SIGNATURE MOVE: Trouble in Paradise

CAREER HIGHLIGHTS: Intercontinental Champion; World Tag Team Champion; United States Champion

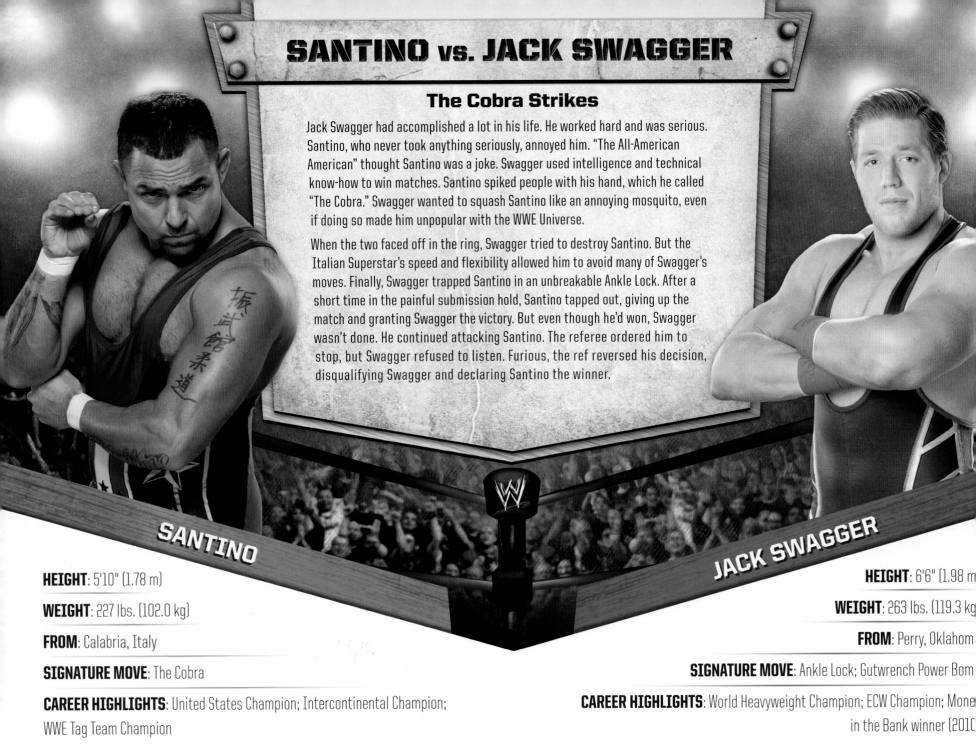

SANTINO vs. JACK SWAGGER

The Cobra Strikes

Jack Swagger had accomplished a lot in his life. He worked hard and was serious. Santino, who never took anything seriously, annoyed him. "The All-American American" thought Santino was a joke. Swagger used intelligence and technical know-how to win matches. Santino spiked people with his hand, which he called "The Cobra." Swagger wanted to squash Santino like an annoying mosquito, even if doing so made him unpopular with the WWE Universe.

When the two faced off in the ring, Swagger tried to destroy Santino. But the Italian Superstar's speed and flexibility allowed him to avoid many of Swagger's moves. Finally, Swagger trapped Santino in an unbreakable Ankle Lock. After a short time in the painful submission hold, Santino tapped out, giving up the match and granting Swagger the victory. But even though he'd won, Swagger wasn't done. He continued attacking Santino. The referee ordered him to stop, but Swagger refused to listen. Furious, the ref reversed his decision, disqualifying Swagger and declaring Santino the winner.

SANTINO

HEIGHT: 5'10" (1.78 m)

WEIGHT: 227 lbs. (102.0 kg)

FROM: Calabria, Italy

SIGNATURE MOVE: The Cobra

CAREER HIGHLIGHTS: United States Champion; Intercontinental Champion; WWE Tag Team Champion

JACK SWAGGER

HEIGHT: 6'6" (1.98 m)

WEIGHT: 263 lbs. (119.3 kg)

FROM: Perry, Oklahom

SIGNATURE MOVE: Ankle Lock; Gutwrench Power Bom

CAREER HIGHLIGHTS: World Heavyweight Champion; ECW Champion; Mone in the Bank winner (2010

KANE vs. RANDY ORTON

The Monster and the Viper

Kane and Randy Orton are both cold-hearted, ruthless men who have no problem hurting their opponents to get a win. And they despise each other. The monstrous Kane is much bigger than Orton, but Orton, known as "The Viper," will fight no matter the size of his foe. Like Kane, he'll do whatever it takes. As the two set their sites on a brawl, the WWE Universe knew it would be exciting—and maybe a little scary—to watch.

The match lived up to expectations. Kane and Orton charged each other, each pummeling his opponent with vicious blows. Orton's smaller size, greater speed, and better agility allowed him to whip his body around Kane, avoiding the Big Red Monster's powerful strikes. Moving quickly, Orton climbed to the top rope and dove off toward his enemy. But the leap failed and Orton landed right in Kane's hands. Kane hoisted the smaller Superstar high into the air, and then crashed him down to the mat with a devastating Chokeslam. Kane won this round, but Orton would fight another day.

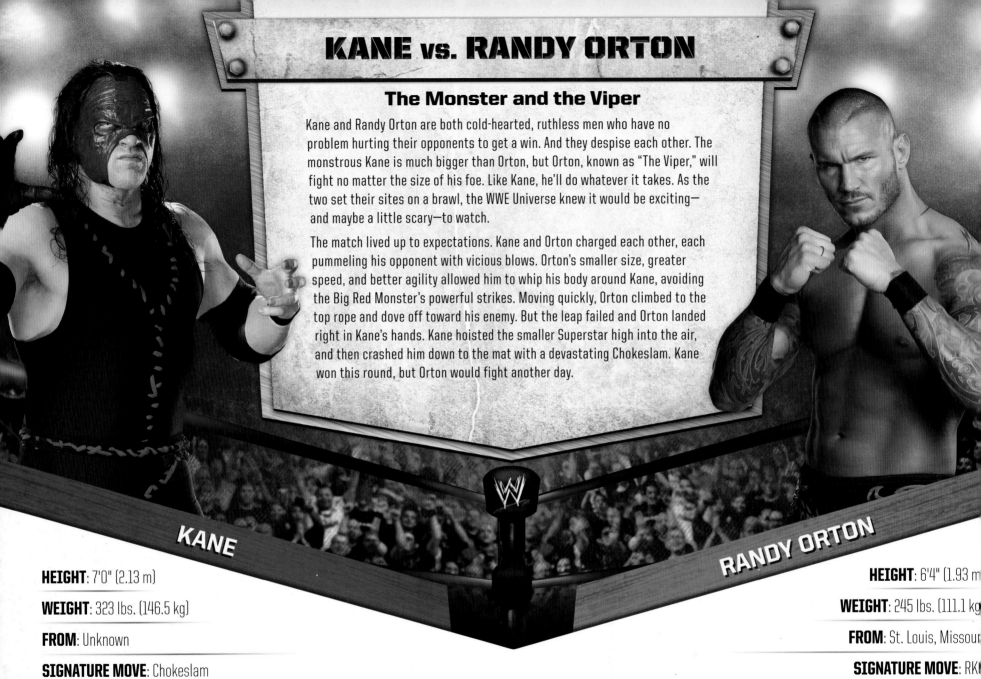

KANE

HEIGHT: 7'0" (2.13 m)

WEIGHT: 323 lbs. (146.5 kg)

FROM: Unknown

SIGNATURE MOVE: Chokeslam

CAREER HIGHLIGHTS: WWE Champion; World Heavyweight Champion; ECW Champion; Intercontinental Champion; World Tag Team Champion; WCW Tag Team Champion; Hardcore Champion

RANDY ORTON

HEIGHT: 6'4" (1.93 m)

WEIGHT: 245 lbs. (111.1 kg)

FROM: St. Louis, Missouri

SIGNATURE MOVE: RKO

CAREER HIGHLIGHTS: WWE Champion; World Heavyweight Champion; Intercontinental Champion; World Tag Team Champion; Royal Rumble Winner (2009)

BRODUS CLAY vs. DOLPH ZIGGLER

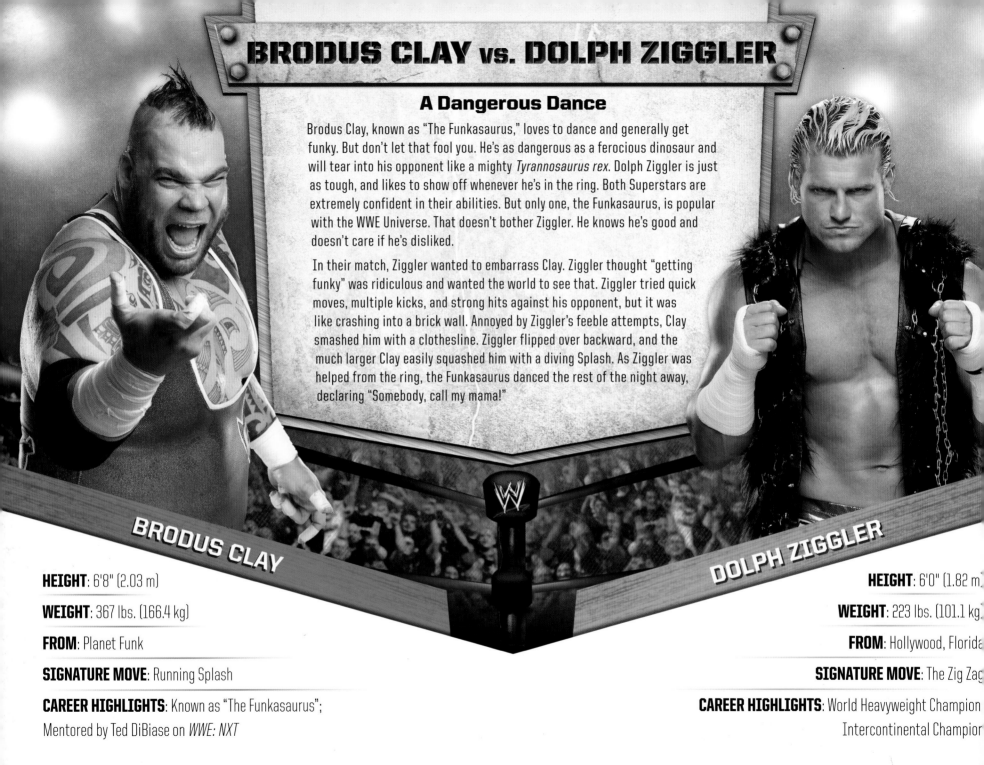

A Dangerous Dance

Brodus Clay, known as "The Funkasaurus," loves to dance and generally get funky. But don't let that fool you. He's as dangerous as a ferocious dinosaur and will tear into his opponent like a mighty *Tyrannosaurus rex*. Dolph Ziggler is just as tough, and likes to show off whenever he's in the ring. Both Superstars are extremely confident in their abilities. But only one, the Funkasaurus, is popular with the WWE Universe. That doesn't bother Ziggler. He knows he's good and doesn't care if he's disliked.

In their match, Ziggler wanted to embarrass Clay. Ziggler thought "getting funky" was ridiculous and wanted the world to see that. Ziggler tried quick moves, multiple kicks, and strong hits against his opponent, but it was like crashing into a brick wall. Annoyed by Ziggler's feeble attempts, Clay smashed him with a clothesline. Ziggler flipped over backward, and the much larger Clay easily squashed him with a diving Splash. As Ziggler was helped from the ring, the Funkasaurus danced the rest of the night away, declaring "Somebody, call my mama!"

BRODUS CLAY

HEIGHT: 6'8" (2.03 m)

WEIGHT: 367 lbs. (166.4 kg)

FROM: Planet Funk

SIGNATURE MOVE: Running Splash

CAREER HIGHLIGHTS: Known as "The Funkasaurus"; Mentored by Ted DiBiase on *WWE: NXT*

DOLPH ZIGGLER

HEIGHT: 6'0" (1.82 m.

WEIGHT: 223 lbs. (101.1 kg.

FROM: Hollywood, Florida

SIGNATURE MOVE: The Zig Zag

CAREER HIGHLIGHTS: World Heavyweight Champion Intercontinental Champion

R-TRUTH vs. EPICO

Rising Stars Falling Fast

Puerto Rico has a long tradition of sports entertainment, and the island has produced some of the greatest Superstars of all time. The latest of these future legends is Epico. Epico is desperate (maybe even too desperate) to carry on the legacy of Puerto Rican power. On this particular day, R-Truth stood in his way. Over the years, R-Truth has drifted in and out of reality, often talking to his unseen friend "Little Jimmy." Epico thinks R-Truth's shaky hold on reality might be the key to victory.

The two opponents locked up in the center of the ring, with the stronger Truth gaining an advantage. Epico tried to go for the ropes so he could launch some aerial moves, but Truth stopped him. Keeping Epico on the ground allowed Truth to launch his own attacks from the sky. Using the ropes to soar through the air, Truth landed a big leg drop on the would-be legend. It was a good strategy, and it put an end to Epico's chances of victory.

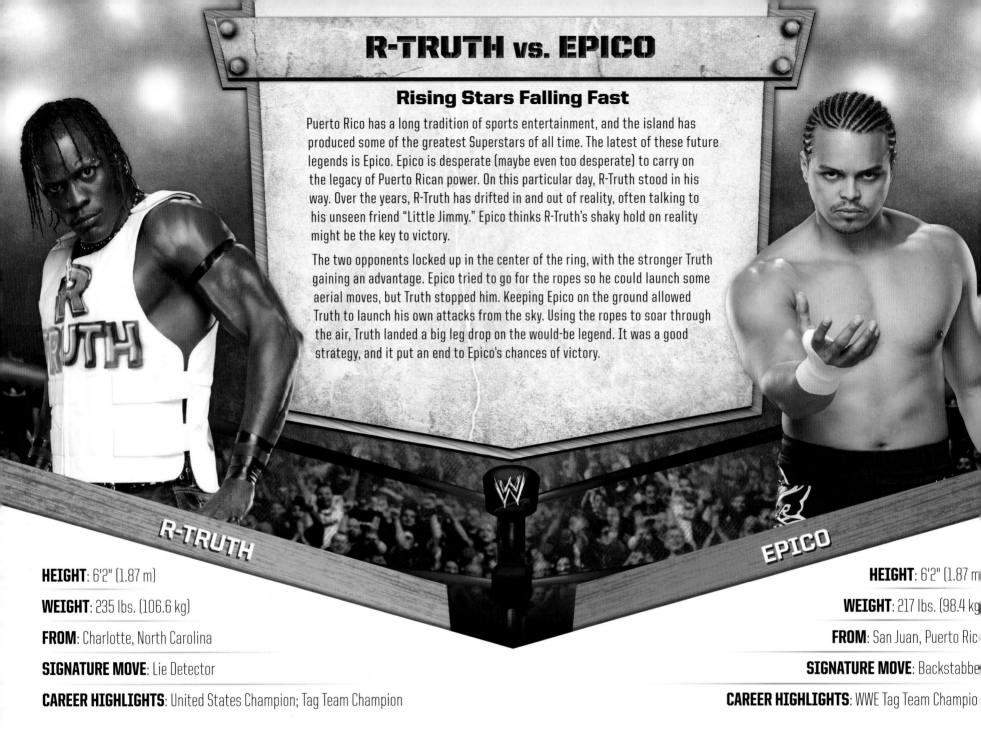

R-TRUTH

HEIGHT: 6'2" (1.87 m)

WEIGHT: 235 lbs. (106.6 kg)

FROM: Charlotte, North Carolina

SIGNATURE MOVE: Lie Detector

CAREER HIGHLIGHTS: United States Champion; Tag Team Champion

EPICO

HEIGHT: 6'2" (1.87 m

WEIGHT: 217 lbs. (98.4 kg

FROM: San Juan, Puerto Ric

SIGNATURE MOVE: Backstabbe

CAREER HIGHLIGHTS: WWE Tag Team Champio

TYSON KIDD vs. YOSHI TATSU

International Incident

Week after week, Tyson Kidd and Yoshi Tatsu exchanged victories in countless battles. Perhaps more than any other pair in the WWE, Kidd and Tatsu are evenly matched. They are the same size, have the same speed, and are equally talented. Tatsu comes from the great Japanese tradition of sports entertainment, while Kidd was the final graduate of the famed Hart Wrestling Dungeon in Calgary, Alberta, Canada. Each feels that their matches are like wrestling a mirror image. It's no wonder these two Superstars have exchanged so many victories.

This match began like all the others, with each man getting in a lot of offense. They countered each other's moves and attacked with their own. It was, as always, back and forth, and totally even. Soon, though, the cheering crowd distracted Tatsu. Kidd leapt into action, forcing Tatsu to the mat and strapping on the devastating Sharpshooter submission hold. Tatsu found the pain too great and quit. Although Kidd won this match, he knew he might not be as lucky next time.

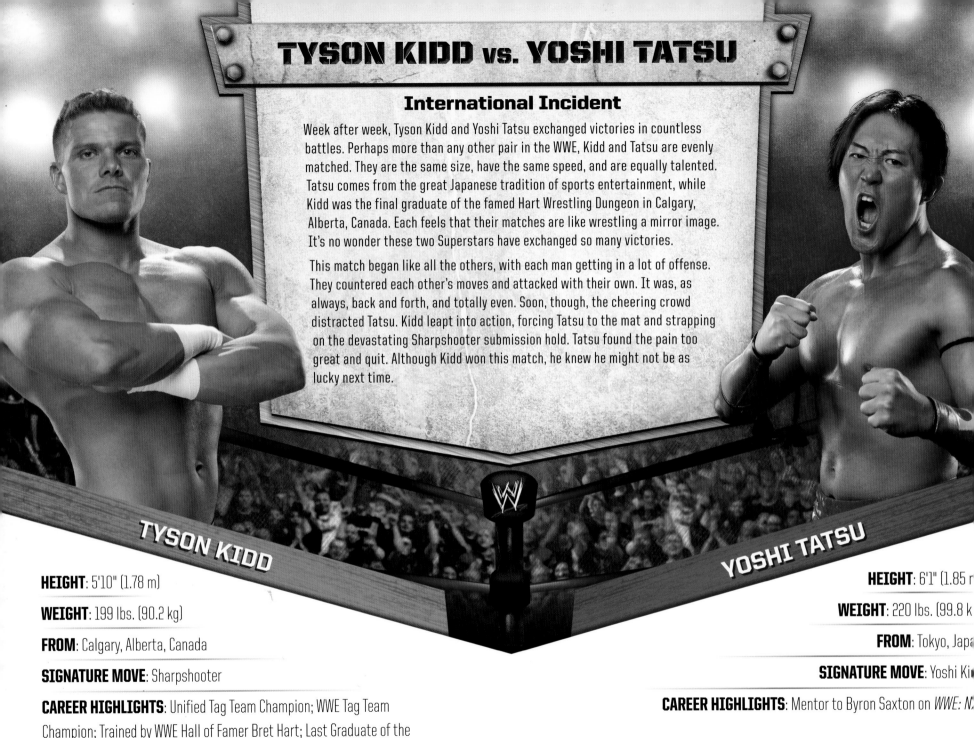

TYSON KIDD

HEIGHT: 5'10" (1.78 m)

WEIGHT: 199 lbs. (90.2 kg)

FROM: Calgary, Alberta, Canada

SIGNATURE MOVE: Sharpshooter

CAREER HIGHLIGHTS: Unified Tag Team Champion; WWE Tag Team Champion; Trained by WWE Hall of Famer Bret Hart; Last Graduate of the Infamous Hart Dungeon

YOSHI TATSU

HEIGHT: 6'1" (1.85 m)

WEIGHT: 220 lbs. (99.8 k

FROM: Tokyo, Japa

SIGNATURE MOVE: Yoshi Ki

CAREER HIGHLIGHTS: Mentor to Byron Saxton on *WWE: N*

ZACK RYDER vs. THE MIZ

Entertainment Value

Both Zack Ryder and The Miz love the spotlight. Ryder created a popular Internet show that gave him thousands of fans and followers. The Miz is the self-proclaimed "Most Must See WWE Champion of All Time," thanks to his appearances on talk shows, reality shows, and of course, the WWE. When they compete in the ring, it's to determine which is the most famous WWE Superstar—at least in the winner's own mind, if not the entire WWE Universe.

When they faced each other, Ryder was waving to his fans, filming them with his phone for his Web show. The Miz snuck up from behind and hit him hard. This early sneak attack gave Miz an advantage that Ryder was never able to overcome. The Miz set up Ryder for his patented finishing move, the Skull-crushing Finale, and drove him to the mat. After a quick three-count, The Miz was declared the winner. Still, Ryder's fans loved him and refused to cheer for the cheating Miz.

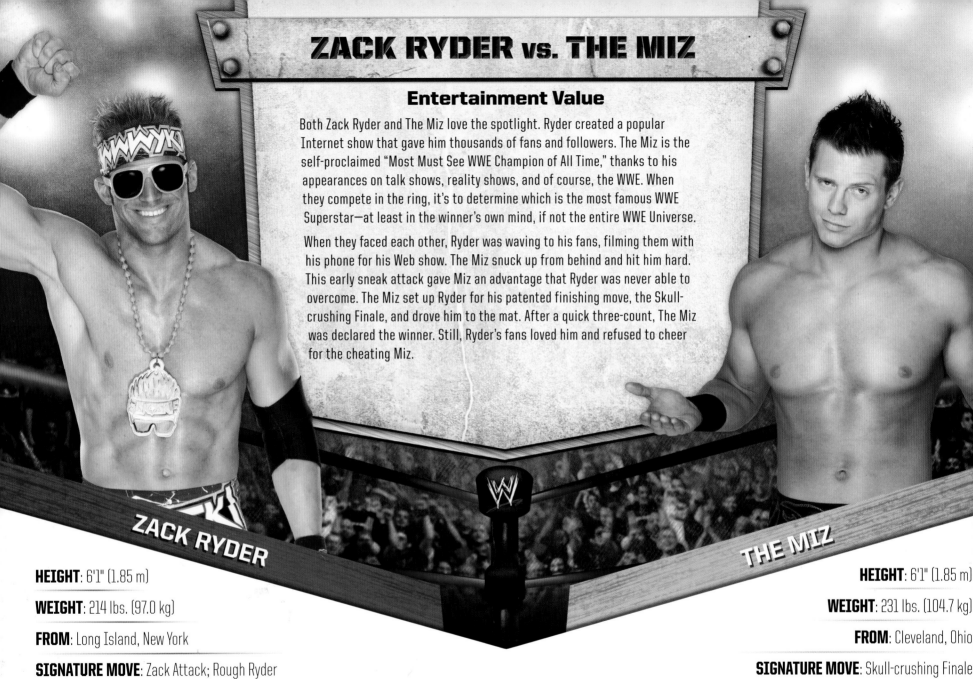

ZACK RYDER

HEIGHT: 6'1" (1.85 m)

WEIGHT: 214 lbs. (97.0 kg)

FROM: Long Island, New York

SIGNATURE MOVE: Zack Attack; Rough Ryder

CAREER HIGHLIGHTS: United States Champion; WWE Tag Team Champion

THE MIZ

HEIGHT: 6'1" (1.85 m)

WEIGHT: 231 lbs. (104.7 kg)

FROM: Cleveland, Ohio

SIGNATURE MOVE: Skull-crushing Finale

CAREER HIGHLIGHTS: WWE Champion; WWE Tag Team Champion; World Tag Team Champion; United States Champion; Raw Money in the Bank Winner (2010)

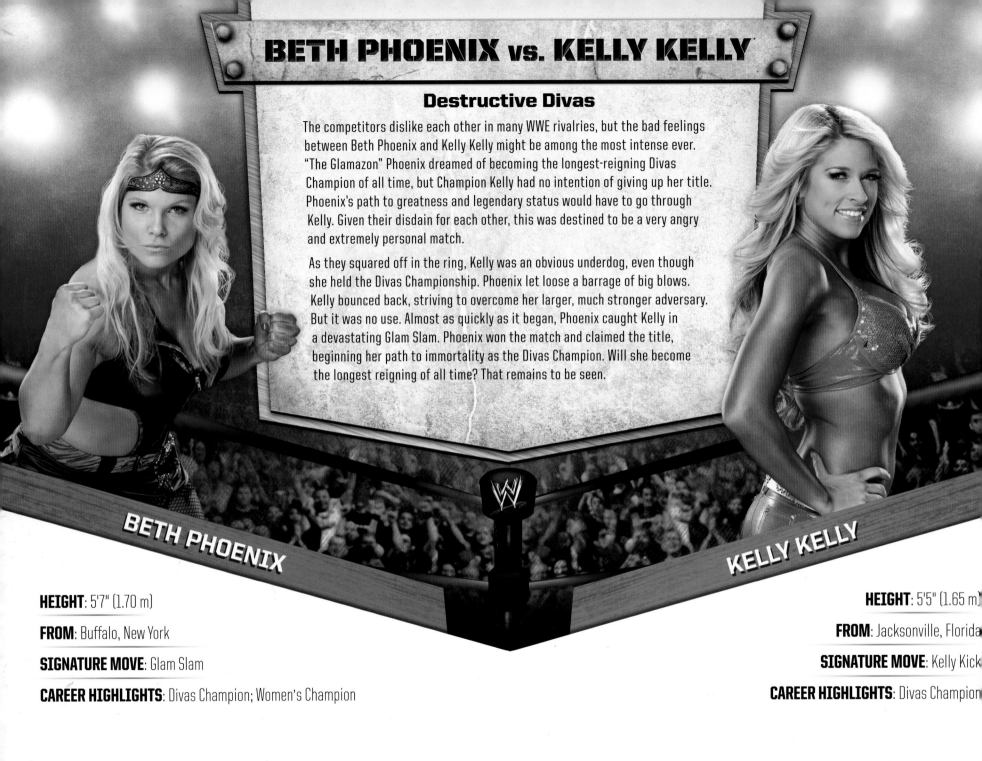

BETH PHOENIX vs. KELLY KELLY

Destructive Divas

The competitors dislike each other in many WWE rivalries, but the bad feelings between Beth Phoenix and Kelly Kelly might be among the most intense ever. "The Glamazon" Phoenix dreamed of becoming the longest-reigning Divas Champion of all time, but Champion Kelly had no intention of giving up her title. Phoenix's path to greatness and legendary status would have to go through Kelly. Given their disdain for each other, this was destined to be a very angry and extremely personal match.

As they squared off in the ring, Kelly was an obvious underdog, even though she held the Divas Championship. Phoenix let loose a barrage of big blows. Kelly bounced back, striving to overcome her larger, much stronger adversary. But it was no use. Almost as quickly as it began, Phoenix caught Kelly in a devastating Glam Slam. Phoenix won the match and claimed the title, beginning her path to immortality as the Divas Champion. Will she become the longest reigning of all time? That remains to be seen.

BETH PHOENIX

HEIGHT: 5'7" (1.70 m)

FROM: Buffalo, New York

SIGNATURE MOVE: Glam Slam

CAREER HIGHLIGHTS: Divas Champion; Women's Champion

KELLY KELLY

HEIGHT: 5'5" (1.65 m)

FROM: Jacksonville, Florida

SIGNATURE MOVE: Kelly Kick

CAREER HIGHLIGHTS: Divas Champion

CHRIS JERICHO vs. BIG SHOW

From Friends to Foes

Chris Jericho and Big Show were once tag team partners, but that team ended a long time ago. While competing together as a team, they learned each other's strengths and weaknesses and used them to win many matches—even the tag team championship. When the team split up, each used his knowledge of the other's abilities to win matches against his former partner.

Despite Big Show's greater size, the two Superstars were evenly matched. Jericho, trained by the famous Hart Family, has tremendous technical ability. He used Big Show's size against him. Remembering Jericho's weaknesses, Big Show took control of the match. But Jericho turned the match in his favor by using technique and intelligence to use leverage on Show's ankles. This forced the giant to drop to the mat. With catlike reflexes and speed, Jericho leapt off the rope in a high backflip called a Lionsault, crashing hard onto the Show and getting the win. Jericho proved, to himself at least, that brains are better than brawn.

CHRIS JERICHO

HEIGHT: 6'0" (1.82 m)

WEIGHT: 226 lbs. (102.5 kg)

FROM: Winnipeg, Manitoba

SIGNATURE MOVE: The Codebreaker; The Walls of Jericho

CAREER HIGHLIGHTS: WWE Champion; World Heavyweight Champion; WCW Champion; Hardcore Champion; World Tag Team Champion; ECW TV Champion; WCW TV Champion; WCW Cruiserweight Champion; Unified Tag Team Champion

BIG SHOW

HEIGHT: 7'0" (2.13 m)

WEIGHT: 485 lbs. (220.0 kg)

FROM: Tampa, Florida

SIGNATURE MOVE: Chokeslam; Knockout Punch; Colossal Clutch

CAREER HIGHLIGHTS: ECW World Champion; WWE Champion; WCW Champion; World Tag Team Champion; WWE Hardcore Champion; United States Champion; WWE Tag Team Champion

BOOKER T vs. CODY RHODES

The Legend and the Kid

For more than two decades, Booker T was one of the all-time greats of sports entertainment. A multi-time world heavyweight champion, Booker T has a history of incredible matches. His "Spinaroonie" is one of the most popular moves in the WWE Universe. Cody Rhodes, the son of WWE Hall of Fame inductee "The American Dream" Dusty Rhodes, had no respect for Booker's accomplishments or skill. For weeks, Rhodes mocked Booker, disrespecting him in public.

Once Booker had had enough, the retired Superstar, now an announcer on SmackDown, sought out his young rival and challenged him to a match. Rhodes appeared to have the early advantage. His youth gave him greater speed and agility, and he knocked Booker off his feet with a single punch. Booker's experience made Rhodes work harder than he had prepared to, but it paid off. The youngster kept the legend down, stomping him back to the mat each time he tried to get up. Rhodes scored a victory, embarrassing Booker T in the process.

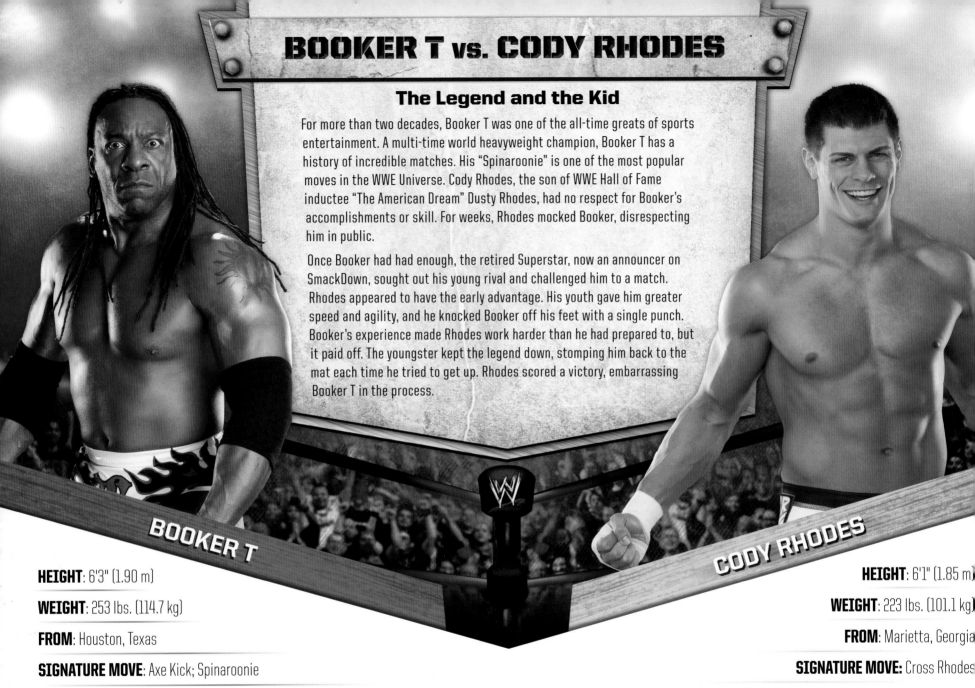

BOOKER T

HEIGHT: 6'3" (1.90 m)

WEIGHT: 253 lbs. (114.7 kg)

FROM: Houston, Texas

SIGNATURE MOVE: Axe Kick; Spinaroonie

CAREER HIGHLIGHTS: World Heavyweight Champion; WCW Champion; World Tag Team Champion; WCW Tag Team Champion; Intercontinental Champion; United States Champion; WCW Television Champion; Hardcore Champion; King of the Ring (2006)

CODY RHODES

HEIGHT: 6'1" (1.85 m)

WEIGHT: 223 lbs. (101.1 kg)

FROM: Marietta, Georgia

SIGNATURE MOVE: Cross Rhodes

CAREER HIGHLIGHTS: Intercontinental Champion; World Tag Team Champion; WWE Tag Team Champion; Son of WWE Hall of Famer "The American Dream" Dusty Rhodes

JUSTIN GABRIEL vs. CURT HAWKINS

Everything to Prove

Justin Gabriel is arguably the most successful WWE Superstar to come from South Africa. A member of the original Nexus, and later of The Corre, the highflying Superstar set out on his own to dominate the WWE. His aerial maneuvers—extremely popular and beautiful to watch—helped him capture the WWE tag team championship. Hawkins had watched the rise of Gabriel with jealousy. After beginning as a sidekick to WWE Hall of Fame inductee Edge, Hawkins assumed his career would skyrocket. But to claim what he felt was rightfully his, Hawkins needed to defeat Gabriel.

Their match was a dream for the WWE Universe. The two Superstars were always exciting in the ring, and their styles complemented each other. Both leapt off the top rope with fast and flying kicks. The brawlers spent more time in the air than on the mat. The match could have gone either way, but this time it was Gabriel who came out on top. His rise toward fame and glory continued, while Hawkins had to wait for another opportunity.

JUSTIN GABRIEL

HEIGHT: 6'1" (1.85 m)

WEIGHT: 223 lbs. (101.1 kg)

FROM: Cape Town, South Africa

SIGNATURE MOVE: 450 Splash

CAREER HIGHLIGHTS: WWE Tag Team Champion; Former member of Nexus and The Corre

CURT HAWKINS

HEIGHT: 6'1" (1.85 m)

WEIGHT: 221 lbs. (100.2 kg)

FROM: Queens, New York

SIGNATURE MOVE: Heat-seeking Elbow

CAREER HIGHLIGHTS: WWE Tag Team Champion

RYBACK vs. HEATH SLATER

Rising Rookies

Ryback, one of the strongest competitors to enter a WWE ring, hits with the force of a speeding truck. He often faces more than one opponent at a time, and he makes quick work of them. A match lasting longer than two minutes is the rare exception for Ryback. Slater isn't as strong as Ryback, but he has a speed advantage and loves competition. The self-proclaimed "One Man Band" was confident in his abilities, and he felt he could handle the mighty Ryback all by himself.

Slater and Ryback's match was surprisingly quick. Well, surprising to Slater. Ryback plowed into Slater like an unstoppable freight train. Slater had no chance to recover, let alone mount any sort of offensive comeback. With an incredible display of strength, Ryback lifted Slater onto his shoulder and marched around the ring. Ryback then slammed Slater down, demonstrating how easy it was for him to defeat an opponent one-on-one. Dragged from the ring by WWE officials, Slater asked if they got the license plate of the truck that hit him. A truck named Ryback!

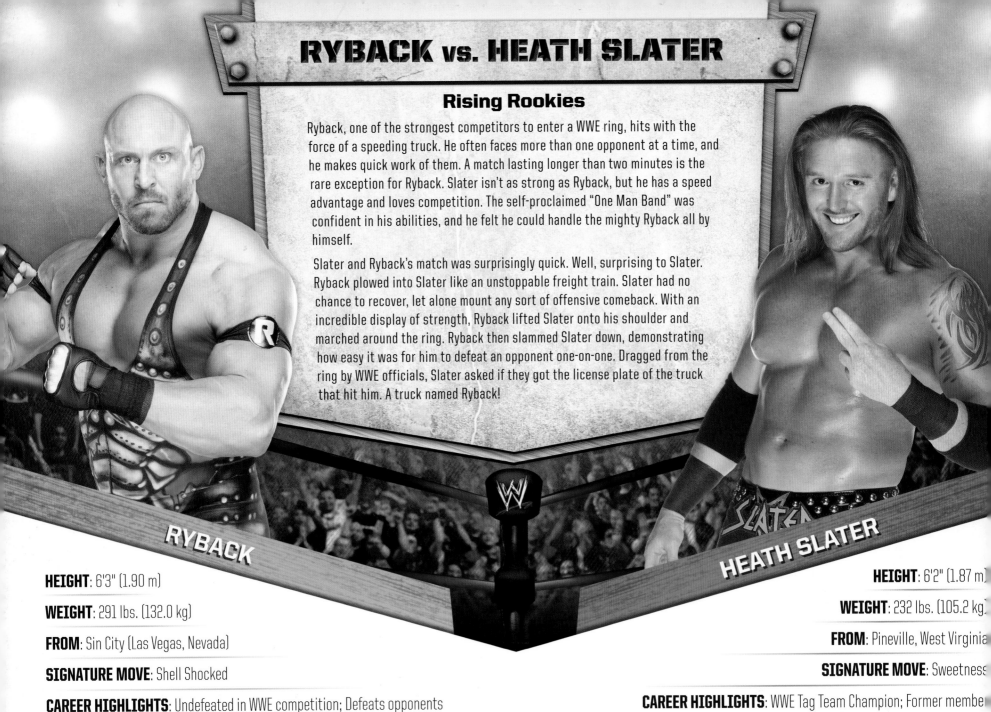

RYBACK

HEIGHT: 6'3" (1.90 m)

WEIGHT: 291 lbs. (132.0 kg)

FROM: Sin City (Las Vegas, Nevada)

SIGNATURE MOVE: Shell Shocked

CAREER HIGHLIGHTS: Undefeated in WWE competition; Defeats opponents in 2-on-1 matches

HEATH SLATER

HEIGHT: 6'2" (1.87 m)

WEIGHT: 232 lbs. (105.2 kg)

FROM: Pineville, West Virginia

SIGNATURE MOVE: Sweetness

CAREER HIGHLIGHTS: WWE Tag Team Champion; Former member of Nexus and The Corre

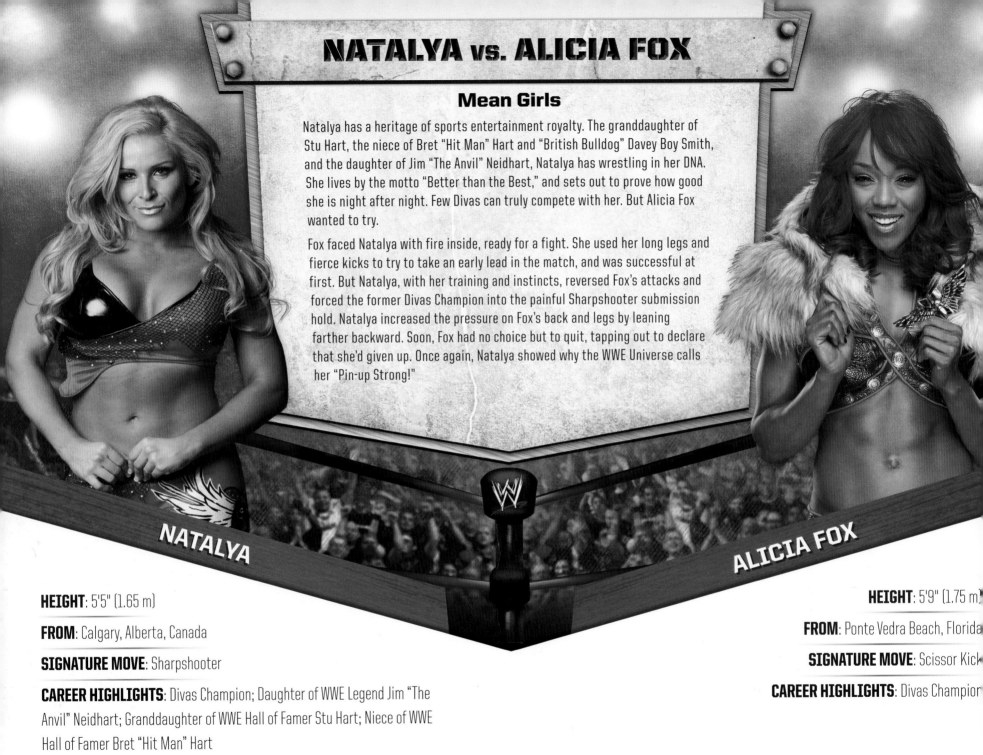

NATALYA vs. ALICIA FOX

Mean Girls

Natalya has a heritage of sports entertainment royalty. The granddaughter of Stu Hart, the niece of Bret "Hit Man" Hart and "British Bulldog" Davey Boy Smith, and the daughter of Jim "The Anvil" Neidhart, Natalya has wrestling in her DNA. She lives by the motto "Better than the Best," and sets out to prove how good she is night after night. Few Divas can truly compete with her. But Alicia Fox wanted to try.

Fox faced Natalya with fire inside, ready for a fight. She used her long legs and fierce kicks to try to take an early lead in the match, and was successful at first. But Natalya, with her training and instincts, reversed Fox's attacks and forced the former Divas Champion into the painful Sharpshooter submission hold. Natalya increased the pressure on Fox's back and legs by leaning farther backward. Soon, Fox had no choice but to quit, tapping out to declare that she'd given up. Once again, Natalya showed why the WWE Universe calls her "Pin-up Strong!"

NATALYA

HEIGHT: 5'5" (1.65 m)

FROM: Calgary, Alberta, Canada

SIGNATURE MOVE: Sharpshooter

CAREER HIGHLIGHTS: Divas Champion; Daughter of WWE Legend Jim "The Anvil" Neidhart; Granddaughter of WWE Hall of Famer Stu Hart; Niece of WWE Hall of Famer Bret "Hit Man" Hart

ALICIA FOX

HEIGHT: 5'9" (1.75 m)

FROM: Ponte Vedra Beach, Florida

SIGNATURE MOVE: Scissor Kick

CAREER HIGHLIGHTS: Divas Champion

DAVID OTUNGA vs. EZEKIEL JACKSON

Brains vs. Brawn

In a classic matchup of brains versus brawn, Harvard-educated lawyer David Otunga set out to face powerhouse Ezekiel Jackson. This is not to say that Otunga has no strength or that Jackson isn't intelligent. Both Superstars have both traits. But Jackson has a little more brawn, while Otunga has a little more brains. Otunga also has a secret weapon. He's the personal legal advisor for John Laurinaitis, general manager of Raw and SmackDown and vice president of talent relations. Otunga knew that, if necessary, Laurinaitis would make the match difficult for Jackson to win.

That's exactly what happened—just as the WWE Universe expected. Jackson was physically more explosive than Otunga, and it looked like Otunga would be pinned. But Laurinaitis interfered, distracting the referee and preventing the three-count. Frustrated by this, Jackson chased Laurinaitis around the ring, until the boss threatened to fire him. The threat gave Otunga his chance to strike. He slammed Jackson onto the mat, pinning his shoulders and earning the victory.

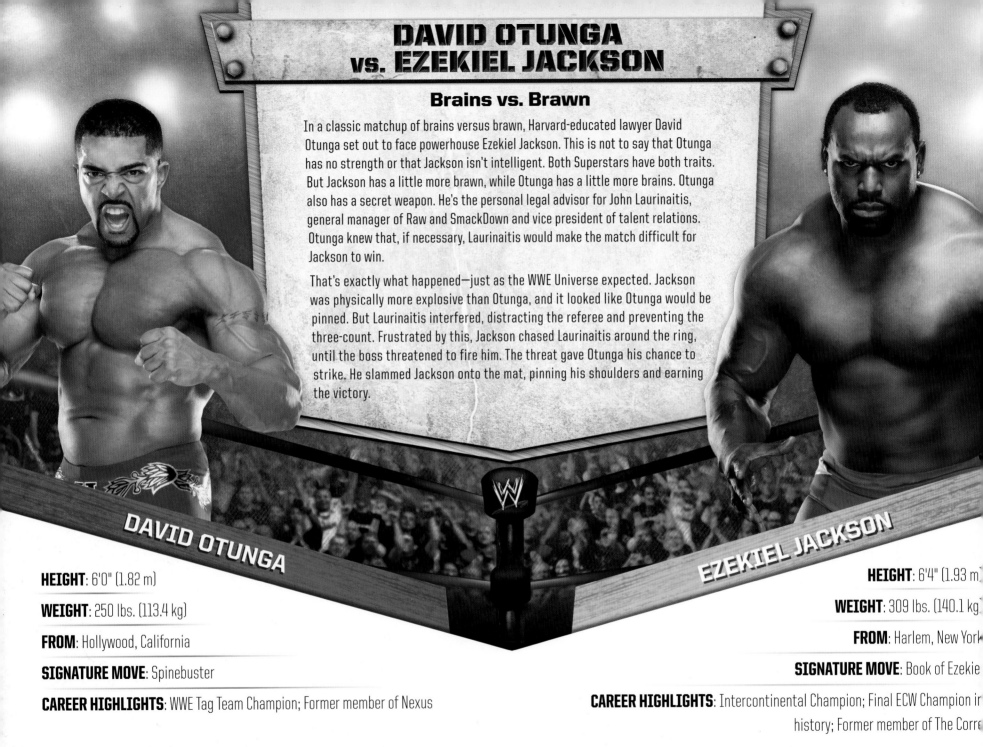

DAVID OTUNGA

HEIGHT: 6'0" (1.82 m)

WEIGHT: 250 lbs. (113.4 kg)

FROM: Hollywood, California

SIGNATURE MOVE: Spinebuster

CAREER HIGHLIGHTS: WWE Tag Team Champion; Former member of Nexus

EZEKIEL JACKSON

HEIGHT: 6'4" (1.93 m)

WEIGHT: 309 lbs. (140.1 kg)

FROM: Harlem, New York

SIGNATURE MOVE: Book of Ezekie

CAREER HIGHLIGHTS: Intercontinental Champion; Final ECW Champion in history; Former member of The Corre

DREW MCINTYRE vs. HORNSWOGGLE

It's All Fun and Games, Until . . .

Hornswoggle is a great mischief-maker, and the WWE Universe loves him for it. But sometimes he goes too far and gets himself into trouble. After pulling a prank on Drew McIntyre, the little leprechaun earned the ire of the "Chosen One." Although the WWE typically would never sanction a match between Hornswoggle and McIntyre, that doesn't mean the two would never collide.

McIntyre convinced WWE to give him a match with the leprechaun. McIntyre was much bigger, and much scarier, but Hornswoggle wouldn't lose easily. As the opening bell rang, he raced out of the ring and slid beneath it, seemingly to disappear. No one knew where he went. Then he reappeared in the ring, behind McIntyre. After Hornswoggle failed at an attempted dive from the top rope, McIntyre slammed his small foe to the mat, defeating him without even breaking a sweat. The WWE Universe was angry at McIntyre for beating Hornswoggle, but McIntyre didn't care. He had put an end to Hornswoggle's mischief—at least for a while.

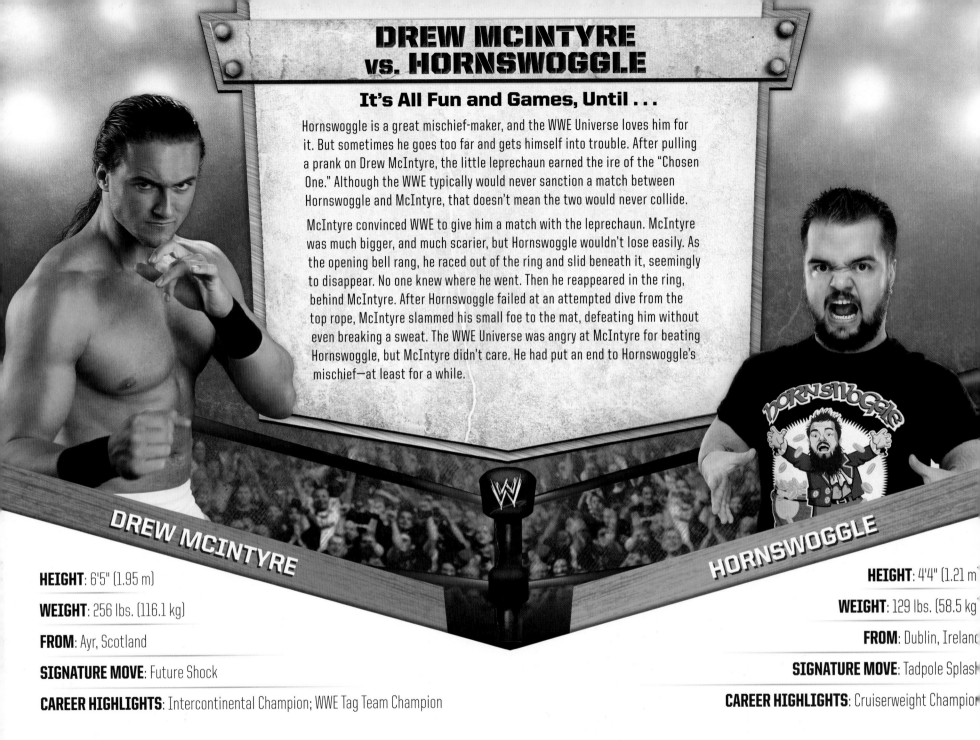

DREW MCINTYRE

HEIGHT: 6'5" (1.95 m)

WEIGHT: 256 lbs. (116.1 kg)

FROM: Ayr, Scotland

SIGNATURE MOVE: Future Shock

CAREER HIGHLIGHTS: Intercontinental Champion; WWE Tag Team Champion

HORNSWOGGLE

HEIGHT: 4'4" (1.21 m)

WEIGHT: 129 lbs. (58.5 kg)

FROM: Dublin, Ireland

SIGNATURE MOVE: Tadpole Splash

CAREER HIGHLIGHTS: Cruiserweight Champion

HUNICO vs. TED DIBIASE

Dueling Dreams

As the son of WWE Hall of Fame inductee "The Million Dollar Man" Ted DiBiase, Sr., Ted DiBiase had everything he could ever desire when he was growing up. This gave him an attitude of entitlement, and by the time he entered WWE, he felt that honors in the world of sports entertainment should be handed to him without his having to work for them. At the other end of the spectrum is Hunico. A talented but angry Superstar from Mexico, Hunico has had to scratch, claw, and fight for everything he's achieved. Seeing DiBiase made him even angrier.

Even though DiBiase reformed his ways and started living the life of a common man, he still had to fight off the threat of an angry Hunico. Hunico attacked with several punches, but DiBiase twisted Hunico's arm, driving the Latino Superstar down. DiBiase tightened his grip, as his newfound fans cheered him on. The pain was too intense and Hunico gave up, but he promised to get his revenge next time.

HUNICO

HEIGHT: 5'10" (1.78 m)

WEIGHT: 205 lbs. (93.0 kg)

FROM: Mexico City, Mexico

SIGNATURE MOVE: Falling Star Splash

CAREER HIGHLIGHTS: 2011 Slammy Award for "Double Vision Moment of the Year"

TED DIBIASE

HEIGHT: 6'3" (1.90 m)

WEIGHT: 235 lbs. (106.6 kg)

FROM: West Palm Beach, Florida

SIGNATURE MOVE: Dream Street

CAREER HIGHLIGHTS: World Tag Team Champion; Son of WWE Hall of Famer "The Million Dollar Man" Ted DiBiase, Sr.; Trained by WWE Hall of Famer Harley Race

MICHAEL MCGILLICUTTY vs. PERCY WATSON

An Explosive Confrontation

Percy Watson started out as a bright young star with a great future ahead of him. As a regular competitor on *WWE: NXT*, he faced other young stars who were as hungry for success as he was. Among them was Michael McGillicutty. A third generation Superstar, McGillicutty was striving to reach the level of "perfection" his father and grandfather had attained during their careers in sports entertainment. As both up-and-coming Superstars began their quests on *NXT*, they both knew that their paths would cross. And it would be explosive.

Both Watson and McGilicutty approached their match with a great will to win, and it showed as they applied wrestling holds and counter holds. Watson leapt out of a hold, ran the ropes, and hit McGillicutty with a big shoulder block. McGillicutty locked him in an armbar and held it tight, Watson crying out in pain. Watson rolled out of the ring, pulling McGillicutty with him. The two Superstars battled outside, neither man making it back inside the ring

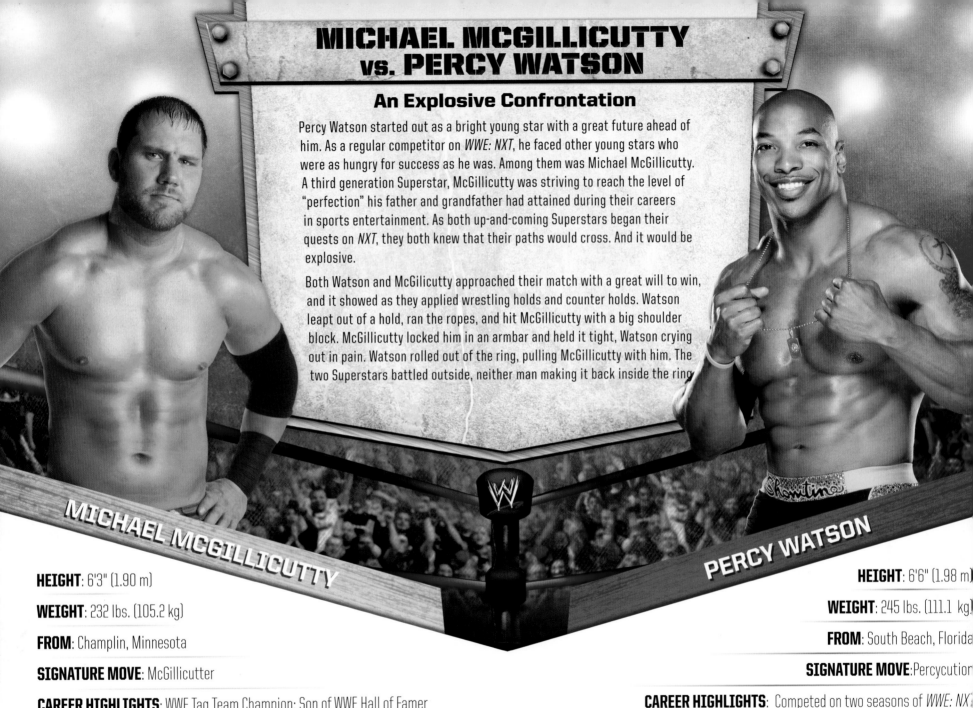

MICHAEL MCGILLICUTTY

HEIGHT: 6'3" (1.90 m)

WEIGHT: 232 lbs. (105.2 kg)

FROM: Champlin, Minnesota

SIGNATURE MOVE: McGillicutter

CAREER HIGHLIGHTS: WWE Tag Team Champion; Son of WWE Hall of Famer "Mr. Perfect" Curt Hennig; Former member of Nexus; Mentored by Kofi Kingston on *WWE: NXT*

PERCY WATSON

HEIGHT: 6'6" (1.98 m)

WEIGHT: 245 lbs. (111.1 kg)

FROM: South Beach, Florida

SIGNATURE MOVE: Percycution

CAREER HIGHLIGHTS: Competed on two seasons of *WWE: NX*

DARREN YOUNG AND TITUS O'NEIL vs. THE USOS

Tag Team Turmoil

Tag team wrestling has a long tradition in WWE. Two Superstars joining forces to prove that they are the best in the world, winning championships, and gaining glory as a team. These goals motivated Titus O'Neil and Darren Young to join forces. But they had a huge obstacle to face in the form of the Usos, twin brothers who carry the legacy of the Samoan people in sports entertainment.

Both teams entered the match with confidence. While the Usos had spent their entire lives together, O'Neil and Young had only recently started teaming. Despite this advantage, the Usos were on the receiving end of a big beating from Young and O'Neil. They were so fast, and hit so hard, the Usos couldn't respond. O'Neil held Jey Uso in a tight, painful bear hug while Young climbed the ropes and slammed Jey with a flying clothesline. The newly formed tag team worked so well together that they effectively double-teamed the Samoan warriors. The Usos lost the match to O'Neil and Young, who were thrilled to be off to such a great start.

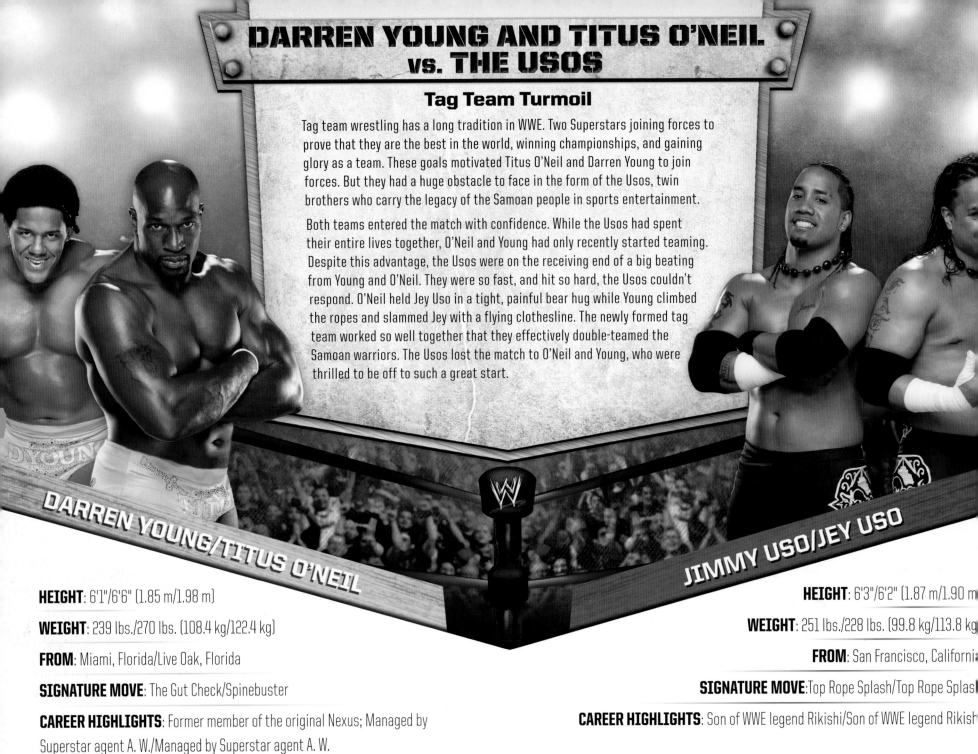

DARREN YOUNG/TITUS O'NEIL

HEIGHT: 6'1"/6'6" (1.85 m/1.98 m)

WEIGHT: 239 lbs./270 lbs. (108.4 kg/122.4 kg)

FROM: Miami, Florida/Live Oak, Florida

SIGNATURE MOVE: The Gut Check/Spinebuster

CAREER HIGHLIGHTS: Former member of the original Nexus; Managed by Superstar agent A. W./Managed by Superstar agent A. W.

JIMMY USO/JEY USO

HEIGHT: 6'3"/6'2" (1.87 m/1.90 m

WEIGHT: 251 lbs./228 lbs. (99.8 kg/113.8 kg

FROM: San Francisco, California

SIGNATURE MOVE: Top Rope Splash/Top Rope Splas

CAREER HIGHLIGHTS: Son of WWE legend Rikishi/Son of WWE legend Rikish

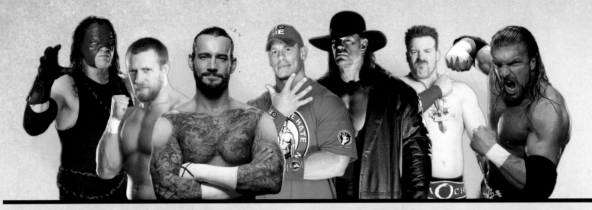

WRESTLEMANIA

WWE puts on more than 300 events around the world every year, but none is more exciting than WrestleMania. For three decades, it has been the largest event in all of entertainment, bringing together top-rated Superstars, Hollywood celebrities, musical pop stars, and more. Every January, when the Road to WrestleMania begins, WWE Superstars compete against one another for the chance to be in the main event. WrestleMania has produced epic matches, including Hulk Hogan vs. Andre the Giant, Shawn Michaels vs. Bret "Hit Man" Hart, Steve Austin vs. The Rock, and CM Punk vs. Chris Jericho.

Held in huge arenas or stadiums, WrestleMania features performances from some of the most popular entertainers in the world. The event grows bigger and becomes better every year. Members of the WWE Universe travel from all over the world to watch WrestleMania live, and every Superstar and Diva strives to compete in the event. It's no wonder that WrestleMania is known as "the showcase of the immortals."